WOMAN'S BEST
FRIEND

~

ALSO BY BARBARA COHEN AND
LOUISE TAYLOR

Dogs and Their Women
Cats and Their Women
Horses and Their Women

❧

SARAH WALSH, LILY, and CHLOE

HAROLD FEINSTEIN

Photographer

WOMAN'S BEST FRIEND

~

A Celebration of
Dogs and Their Women

BARBARA COHEN AND
LOUISE TAYLOR

LITTLE, BROWN AND COMPANY
Boston   New York   Toronto   London

For Gabe and Glory

FIRST EDITION

Excerpt from the Introduction, *Animals . . . Our Return to Wholeness* © 1993 by Penelope Smith (Pegasus Publications, P.O. Box 1060, Point Reyes, CA 94956). Reprinted by permission of the author.
Photograph on page 18 from *Rosie, a Visiting Dog's Story* by Stephanie Calmenson, Clarion Books, New York. Reprinted by permission of the author.

ISBN 0-316-15054-1

Library of Congress Catalog Card Number 96-75393

10 9 8 7 6 5 4 3

RRD-VA

Designed by Barbara Werden

Published simultaneously in Canada by Little, Brown & Company (Canada) Limited

PRINTED IN THE UNITED STATES OF AMERICA

ACKNOWLEDGMENTS

~

WE ARE tremendously grateful to the women and photographers included in *Woman's Best Friend* whose efforts made the book possible. Special thanks to the hundreds of women across the country who also sent letters, stories, and photographs expressing their unconditional love of dogs — their spirit and enthusiasm appear on every page.

We are indebted to Rose Marston and Ren Norton for providing the photograph for our flyer of Rose with Livingston, which gave the project a jump start. Heartfelt thanks to our dear friend Margie Arnold, who has been so generous and supportive with all four books, and to our families and friends who were there when we needed them.

We'd like to thank the following organizations and individuals for helping spread the word about *Woman's Best Friend: The Advocate;* Gerry Azata; *Provincetown Banner;* Boston Animal Rescue League; *Canine Grapevine; InterActions,* a Delta Society Publication; *Dogworld; DOG FANCY; Provincetown Magazine;* Jane M. Rohman; South Shore Humane Society; *Tailwaggers; Tuftonia;* Cristin Merck of Tufts University School of Veterinary Medicine; and *The Women's Review of Wellesley.*

For helping in their own special way we extend thanks to Suzy Becker, Bonnie Bergin, the staff at the DeCordova Museum and Sculpture Park (especially Susan Diachisin), Ellie Garber, Peg Hall, Brielle Kay, Honey Black Kay, Perceptions, the postal staffs of Provincetown and Stow, Massachusetts, Carol Ross, Chris Triebert, and Marian Roth, Mary De Angelis, Paul Churchill, and Karen Harding, who always took care of Gabe.

Colleen Mohyde gave us encouragement and valuable guidance throughout the project, for which we're most grateful. And many thanks to Abigail Wilentz at Little, Brown for her important assistance, to our copyeditor, Betty Power, and to our editor, Jennifer Josephy, for her belief in our four books, especially *Woman's Best Friend*.

Finally we salute the ones who give unconditional love and buoy us with their joyful spirits and zest for life — our dogs, Gabe and Glory; unknowingly, they have given the most.

INTRODUCTION

~

WHAT IS IT about dogs that captures women's hearts so tenaciously? In 1989 we explored the question with our first book, *Dogs and Their Women*. Although years have passed since its publication, the response has never ceased. We continue to receive letters and comments from women who indicate that *Dogs and Their Women* is their "all-time favorite book," and that "If you ever do another one, I want to be in it." Some, grieving the loss of a dog, found great solace in the collection of photographs and stories. Others express the significant role dogs play in their lives as nothing short of a passion.

Of course we've always felt passionate about our dogs, whether they were hanging their smiling faces out car windows, ears streaming in the wind, or lying underfoot in our kitchens. We know there is nothing more gratifying than a dog's unconditional love, no truer friend, better playmate, or comforting shoulder. There's enormous joy in observing them close up or from afar. Barbara often tells the story about seeing Gabe being towed on a surfboard around Provincetown Harbor as she looked out her window one summer morning. And Louise attests to nothing more poetical than watching Glory meander about the apple orchard, her black tail barely visible above the tall green grass.

The abundance of canine love, combined with the response to *Dogs and Their Women,* continually fueled our creative spirits. Consequently, we decided to collect another group of photographs and stories about the remarkable and intimate relationships with woman's best friend.

While compiling the manuscript, our emotions constantly fluctuated between joy and sorrow indicating dogs' greatest gift. For, we believe, in order to live life to the fullest — to live with dogs — we must be willing to experience and rejoice in the full range of feelings they evoke.

The women and dogs you'll meet here come from more than twenty-five states. There's Trooper, the greyhound collie with a gallant heart who competes in a local Mutt Derby; and Winston, the yellow Lab who destroys practically everything in sight and still manages to be loved. Claudia Tokuyama-Hack shares not only her pack of beautiful dogs, but wisdom about their short lives, and the fear of loss we grapple with as they grow older. And then there's Meko, a terrific little Montana mutt who helps Ellen Raines open the doors of her hearing-impaired world and wins her heart over as well. Describing her seasonal adventures with Chevy, the Dog of Dogs, Jay Rancourt's exuberance nearly leaps off the page. They sled pell-mell down her steep, icy driveway, kayak wild rivers in summer, and skim lakes so still you can hear the loons calling.

We could go on and on about dogs and their women, produce a similar book year after year, and never feel the subject's been overdone. But for now, turn the pages and find a delightful selection of wonderful canines and their faithful female companions.

Woman's Best Friend is a testament to the nature and spirit of women who choose to live with dogs. It is a reminder to salute those gentle souls who comfort with soft muzzles, pull us through screen doors into the fresh air, stop the chatter in our heads by a wagging tail or by dropping tennis balls at our feet. We hope you'll find an aspect of you and your dog on every page.

WOMAN'S BEST FRIEND

~

MARILYN BURNETT, JESSE, and TEXAS

~

If I know only one thing for certain, it's this: Without them, I would be something different, something less, someone else.

JOHN BRINKMAN
Photographer

JAY RANCOURT and CHEVY

❧

I CAN SEE HER in my mind's eye on our early-morning constitutionals up the east shore of Moosehead Lake. I in my racy sea kayak and she streaking along the shore, ears flying, long strides, big grin, tongue flopping about — the picture of canine joy. After a week or so of daily exercise, she'll run fifteen miles, swimming all the inlets, outswimming every dog she encounters. Then she'll sleep the rest of the day and evening, dreaming in the sun. But if she hears the scrape of a boat on beach gravel, or a car door opening, or a bicycle wheel ticking over, she's on her feet and ready. The next morning when the first rays of sun slant into the inlet, I'll see her from the kitchen window, curled up on the deck of the sunfish or sitting in the forward seat of the double kayak, listening to the loons and waiting for a ride.

I worry about her sometimes. She is a dog who would rather die than be left behind. Literally. I know she would follow me anywhere. A few summers ago we sailed twenty miles in the little sunfish. She'd fall asleep on the deck, and a gust of wind would spill her sound asleep into the water. With a little help from me she'd clamber back on and, unperturbed, fall asleep in moments. Then another gust would come along . . .

In winter I can whistle her onto the front of the runner sled for a wild ride down the icy driveway. I've landed on her so many times I expect her to balk, but she never does. I made her a harness so she could pull me along the railroad tracks on my cross-country skis. She'll pull me for a while with gusto and when she gets tired of it, she sits down until I release her. Then she's off with a bound, looking

over her shoulder to see if I'm following. She prefers to be in front of me and will chitter loudly if I get ahead of her.

She is so fit from all the exercise, people think she's a puppy. She's nearly seven years old! Chevy, the Dog of Dogs!

LICHEN RANCOURT
Photographer

5

JOHANNA FINKLE, DODGER, and CLANCY

~

I
T'S TOUGH WHEN you love dogs as much as I do and have terrible allergies. That's why I have my hypoallergenic sweethearts. *No,* they are not poodles; they are Irish water spaniels, also known as "the clowns of the spaniel family."

Dodger loves chasing my rabbit, Lopsy, around the house and has developed a taste for my favorite stuffed animals. He makes up for all his bad habits when I am sick and spends the days cuddled with me on the couch — even though he insists on having the pillow and blanket for himself.

Clancy is Dodger's older half-brother. His hobbies are playing with tennis balls and stealing my socks. All in all, my two curly clowns are the best friends I have.

SANDRA MONGEON
Photographer

KARYN ZUBA REASONER and BEN

~

W E WANTED TO TALK ABOUT how special we are to each other and how we are best friends and soul mates. But instead we decided to share the top ten questions and comments we receive when we go to the park.

10. Where's that barrel thing under his neck?

9. Is he walking you or are you walking him?

8. How much does he eat?

7. Can I ride him?

6. Does he bite?

5. That's a big dog, ain't it?

4. He's bigger than you!

3. What's wrong with his lips?

2. Is he that Cujo dog?

1. Look! It's Beethoven!

RICHARD MICHAEL REASONER
Photographer

SOPHIA PELAEZ and CLANCEY

M Y NAME IS CLANCEY and the woman in the photo with me is Sophia. Two years ago Sophia had a stroke, lost her short-term memory, and had to move in with her daughter Lori and me.

One day Lori suspected Sophia was suffering from irregularity and gave her a mild laxative. The problem came a few hours later at the beach. Thinking the real harm could be to Sophia's self-esteem, I sprang into action before anyone realized what was going on. I took off down the beach to where a family was setting up their beach blanket. Lori chased after me, yelling, and just when she got within good visual contact, I started pooping in a pair of shoes on the family's blanket. Lori was simply stunned, Sophia was wondering what was going on, and the family thought they had gotten into a circus sideshow.

Lori had the good sense to take us home. Once in the privacy of our home Sophia's problem became apparent, and Lori was stunned again. The environment was rather glum, and I wondered whether my performance had been the right tack. After an hour or so, Lori stopped what she was doing and said to Sophia, "All I wanted was some quiet time at the beach and you pooped in your pants and Clancey pooped in someone's shoes. I just don't believe it!" Sophia looked up and said, "Well, I guess that's what's called a real shitty time at the beach!" They both looked at me, then at each other, and finally broke out laughing. The glum mood was over at last.

L. M. PELAEZ
Photographer

CHERYL COOK and CLOVIS

~

THE DAY AFTER the adoption, Clovis was exploring every blade of grass and leaf in my front yard, which drops off steeply to a pond. When she disappeared, I heard a splash and thought my eight-week-old puppy was going to drown. I raced barefoot to the hill and down through the twigs, leaves, and plants. Halfway there I saw her and stopped. A very happy puppy was swimming with the mallards.

ROGER BARNABY
Photographer

JILL M. POTTLE, GARTH, and CARLOS

∾

O NCE YOU PICK A BREED and form an attachment, the special characteristics they possess become endearing and irreplaceable. It seems silly and biased to fall in love this way, but the process is inescapable.

My dogs, of course, are the best in the world and among the smartest and most handsome of all breeds. Carlos, my six-year-old German shepherd, is big and black with intense chestnut-colored eyes. People think he's part wolf. Although he appears ominous, Carlos is more of a lounge dog, and he likes everybody.

Demanding my constant attention and guidance is my five-month-old standard poodle, Garth. He's electrified, interacting with everyone and everything, including the full-length mirror. He'll stop in front of it, stare at himself intensely, then bark, feign attack, and run away expecting to be chased. I like joining the game and stand behind him pretending I'm going to pounce. He loves this.

Carlos and Garth bring magic to my life as an artist. They are the crème de la crème when it come to humor, personality, and ability to entertain me for hours. How can you beat that?

DAVID CARAS
Photographer

© David Caras

PENELOPE SMITH and PASHA

~

MOST INVESTIGATIONS into interspecies communication are still mainly concerned with communicating with animals indirectly: getting them to learn our symbols and communicate in human language, or respond to our cues. However, there is a growing realization, an awakening cultural awareness, that we are all linked — physically, mentally, and spiritually. The attitude that receiving thought-communication from animals is just childish imagination and projection is shifting.

The telepathic link has been there throughout the ages, veiled by our disrespect and ignorance. Beliefs about animals' lack of ability have inhibited and suppressed human understanding. It is possible that our damage to the planet's ecosystem and our lopsided relationship with the rest of nature, which is mainly caused by human ideas of separation, dominance, and superiority, may be largely resolved through interspecies respect and understanding.

I have been communicating with animals telepathically all my life, doing counseling and healing work with animals and their people since 1971 and offering books, tapes, and workshops. I rejoice in the burgeoning awareness that has encouraged many people to rediscover, develop, and use their interspecies telepathic abilities.

JIM CRAVEN
Photographer

16

ASHA IMAN VEAL and GEORGETTE

～

Georgette was there when I needed her through my parents' divorce. Even when my family was changing, she remained the same. I don't know if she knew how much she helped me or how happy she made me, but she did a great job of it.

GAY CURRIER
Photographer

SUSAN FLEISHER and GEORGE

~

GEORGE FOLLOWED AIRPLANES across the sky, and the flight of birds. She was the most visual dog I ever knew, and her sense of sight translated into protective behavior. If I placed a Christmas card on the mantel, hung a new photograph on the wall or moved one to a different place, I would soon hear a low, fierce growl, and find her crouched in front of it. What she wanted was an explanation that the object wasn't going to harm me. She responded like this to most anything new, and I became accustomed to showing and naming for her whatever I brought into the house.

Late one night, with a very persistent *woof, woof,* she woke me and led me downstairs into the kitchen. The toaster oven had short-circuited and was glowing red with heat. The plastic knobs were too hot to touch, as were the cabinets above and the tile countertop. Using pot holders, I tossed the whole thing into the stove oven, kissed George, and thanked her for protecting me.

Although I have been a daughter, wife, and mother, I've never felt so well loved and so loving until George shared my life. George died of a genetic disease at twenty-one months. She was the dog of my life, and I miss her beyond telling.

ALBERT R. LEVY
Photographer

DEBORAH DAY HUGHES, TRAVELLER, and IRENE

~

A CLOUDY, COLD mid-November day, in my estimation, is the best time to go to the shore of Lake Michigan with Irene and Traveller, my Scottish deerhounds. We'll pile into the car with camera, coffee thermos, and water for the dogs. I know we'll have the beach to ourselves.

This day the dogs discovered how much fun it was to run to the top of the dune and come hurtling down. It looked so exhilarating, I decided to join them. As I ran down the dune, my feet were supported by the heavy sand, yet the sensation came close to that of flying. We fell, rolled, ran up and down again and again, trying to come close to each other without tripping. Eventually we wore ourselves out and stopped to rest in the crusty, scrambled sand.

DAN GAUSS
Photographer

23

PAMELA JEAN TAYLOR-SHEPPECK
and MIMSEY ROSEBUD

❧

IT WAS FREEZING at the National Seashore on Cape Cod. Wearing only shorts and a tank top, I grabbed Mimsey's sheet from the car to wrap around me. We walked along the beach, my teeth chattering while Mimsey splashed slowly and happily through the dark blue water on her three sturdy legs. When I sat down to get out of the wind, she lay beside me, pushed the sheet up with her nose, crawled under it, and maneuvered herself around me like a cocoon. It should have been comforting — her big body pressed against mine — the two of us sharing each other's warmth. But my goofy, cosy Mimsey took up most of the sheet and was caked with cold, wet sand.

When Mimsey was diagnosed with osteosarcoma, she trusted me to fight the disease aggressively with the latest treatments. She knew when to say "no more," and make me understand. I hope when it's my time, I have the integrity to go with it like my Mimz.

RICK SHEPPECK
Photographer

NAN FOSTER, BERTHA, and BEULAH MARIE

∽

ERTHA AND I relax in our field after a long day of work at a children's trauma clinic. She's our resident canine social worker on Mondays, and all the kids love her. Sometimes I wonder if she isn't overextended. This week, in addition to her regular duties, she had three rehearsals in my fifth-grader's musical production of *Annie*. As she plays the part of Sandy, no one seems to mind that she's a black instead of a yellow dog. Her dynamic personality has obviously worked its way into the hearts of teachers and students alike.

In the background is her daughter, Beulah Marie. She's impatiently awaiting some form of action. Her week has been less tiring, bringing in kindling for the wood stove on every walk. Beulah Marie is the designated mascot for the local hockey team and has been known to take an overly active role in most practices. Joyfully stealing the puck, she especially enjoys the ensuing chase! At home her teeth remain busy, leaving her insignia on shoes, socks, and furniture.

I've come to the conclusion life would be a bit dull without these two busy bees.

JEANNINE BRETON
Photographer

JANE M. ROHMAN and JACK

❧

MY BEAUTIFUL BIG BOY faithfully wakes me with his wet nose nudging mine, his red leash hanging from his mouth, and his tail wagging so furiously that I sometimes call him Elvis. Before I got Jack, I was an unattached thirty-two-year-old business executive with a seemingly brilliant advertising career. Truth be known, I was miserable and dreadfully lonely. After years of exotic travel, long work nights, and too many Casanovas, I wanted to plant some real roots. After much debate over the fairness of city living for a dog, I brought home Jack, a seventeen-pound pup.

Jack transformed me. He brought back what my mom used to say was the old Jane — the one with an air of optimism and an easy laugh.

My near-obsession with Jack and giving him a good life, despite our city environs, gave me the idea for my canine guidebook, *The Dogs' Guide To New York City with Jack, The City Dog.*

I believe it was no coincidence that while working on the book with Jack at my side, I found the greatest man in the world. Besides loyalty and companionship, Jack has given me the gift of love.

WALTER BREDEL
Photographer

ELLEN RICHAU RAINES and MEKO

MEKO WAS the first hearing ear dog placed by the Dogs for the Deaf in Montana. Isolated, angry, and frustrated, I applied for a hearing ear dog with hopes it would help me accept my deafness and alleviate the struggles I faced everyday. After waiting eighteen months, I received an ugly, wispy-haired, twelve-pound mutt with bat-like ears. I was disappointed and wondered what had I gotten myself into. I didn't want this dog but knew it was time to live a normal life. After the trainer encouraged me to give myself a chance, Meko was let off her leash to explore what would be her new home.

Our day started with many sounds and rewards. Meko was happy working for me. She trailed me everywhere on her short, dainty legs, and was busy transferring both her authority and affection. This made me uneasy. I didn't know if I could handle being labeled deaf, which Meko will do by just being with me.

Soon we were out of the house taking daily walks and mingling with the public. People were uneducated about service dogs, and angry that Meko was in grocery stores and other public places with them. Though I hated confrontation, I became determined Meko had a right to be with me wherever I went.

Many battles ensued, but gradually we made progress and even began giving demonstrations to children and organizations all over Montana. I'm so proud of Meko for helping me open doors. I no longer think she's ugly. How can I when she's so beautiful?

LARRY STANLEY
Photographer

DELTA SOCIETY
1994
SERVICE DOG
OF
THE YEAR
Hearing

Presented to
Ellen Raines
and
Meko

Sponsored by
Hill's Pet Nutrition, Inc.

© 1995 Larry Stanley Photography

KAREN VAN ALLSBURG
and MISS JANE

~

How I love my dear Jane Doe. Abandoned in Maine's muddy springtime, she was rescued by a neighbor who discovered her wandering with a face full of porcupine quills.

Mine was the first name on the list of possible parents. I love dogs of all descriptions and am ever ready to take care of those belonging to others.

My first glimpse of her, I must confess, was a bit of a disappointment — I had been imagining a golden or Labrador retriever. There she was, timid, shaking, with a pointy black-freckled nose, long, skinny legs, and a curled white tail, which, she later demonstrated, she could twirl like a helicopter propeller. Her soft, velvet black ears lay close to her head, and she looked at me with dark brown eyes that knew so much.

I borrowed her for a weekend, felt uncertain, returned her. I borrowed her again — we bonded. Thus began a profoundly enriched and entertaining journey — life with Miss Jane Doe.

ANN HOPPS
Photographer

ROSE MARSTON and LIVINGSTON

~

THE FIRST TIME I went to his house, I fell in love with him. Oh, I eventually fell in love with his owner as well, whose Afghan hound, normally leery of people, had immediately taken to me. I had simply greeted Livingston with a great big "Hi!" — the same way I greet all dogs.

Thinking over the last seven years with Livingston, I'm awed by his diversity of character. When I arrive home, he wags his curly tail, comes over and leans against me. He's not interested in dog things like sticks, balls, and biscuits, but in his younger days he had no problem getting up on the kitchen counter. Oh, he's bad all right, and as charming as a used car salesman. He talks with his eyes, steals your heart, and steals the sausage right off your plate.

Livingston used to be like a child, the bad boy, but now he's thirteen and it's like watching my parents die again. Every morning I brace myself before going downstairs, fearing today is the day he didn't make it through the night. He has this tremendous independent will to keep going.

ON NOVEMBER 20, 1995, Livingston didn't make it through the night, but he'll always be a part of the pack.

REN NORTON
Photographer

STEPHANIE CALMENSON
and ROSIE

∼

COME ON, ROSIE. Bring the stick to me!" I call.

We're on the beach. It's just the two of us, but it won't be for long. Soon kids will start wandering over. They always do. That's because Rosie is kid-size and kid-friendly. And she's got all this hair hanging over her eyes. Makes her mysterious . . .

"How can she see?" the kids ask. "Does she do tricks?" "How old is she?" "Does she bite?" "Can I see her teeth?"

I answer all their questions. The next thing I know, they're playing with my dog, I'm talking to their parents, and thanks to Rosie, we're a whole new circle of friends.

JUSTIN SUTCLIFFE
Photographer

© Justin Sutcliffe

JUDY JORDAN FLATEN
and PADDINGTON

$\backsim$

MY CONCERN for homeless dogs led me to the local humane society to walk them whenever I could. At the end of the kennel there was a huge pup I was told not to walk. He had large bumps on his legs, a condition called hypertrophic osteodystrophy, and the outlook was dim. I decided if walking was out of the question, TLC certainly wasn't. As I crouched beside him, he looked up at me with long, liquid eyes, then tripped over his big feet to crawl into my lap and bury his head.

Paddington is now five years old, with straight, strong legs, and weighs 135 pounds. There has never been a dog like my Paddington. He is part of my soul.

SUSAN NEWBERRY
Photographer

BRIELLE KAY and LOUIE

～

WHEN LOUIE WAS A PUPPY, he had little skunk eyes that slanted like Zorro's mask. His fur was soft as a rabbit's, and I used to let him sleep on the bed with me. This was a mistake because he got bigger and bigger. Eventually I moved to the floor and he stayed on my bed. Then I got another bed, so we each had one of our own.

When he wanted to sleep on my new bed, I kicked him out of the room. Then I had to barricade the doors with furniture because he learned how to open them. If he couldn't get in the room at night, he'd hold a grudge against me for at least a week.

You see, he was used to being the king. When we took walks, though, he was really more like a movie star. Everyone had to stop, admire and pat him, and ask thousands of questions.

Louie will always be my dog, even though I don't live with him anymore. He's happy in his new home, a farm in North Carolina, on the side of a mountain. He's got a blind dog and a goat for friends, and now he's able to be a real dog and go for uninterrupted walks.

SACHA A. RICHTER
Photographer

MIRIAM CUTLER and NIKI LOUISE

⮯

N IKI'S GOT TONS of "doggie-nality," and knows how to savor life's little moments, whether chewing on a smelly old bone she's just dug up from the yard, "rooffy-rooffing" around sensuously on the rug, or discovering yet another adorable lounging position in her bed. I envy her unfettered existentialism. She's just as excited about going into the house as she was going out in the first place. Even a two-minute ride — just to move the car — is great cause for jubilation.

SHERRY RAYN BARNETT
Photographer

DEBBY RUSSEL, SHERMAN, and CHUMLEY

～

EACH MORNING we plow the woodland trails. We anticipate this hike for different reasons. I seek physical and spiritual exercise, they simply want a chance to sniff! Although I am the leader of this pack, the path we take is often determined by a nose. We scramble over stone walls, wade through streams, and explore deer runs. I watch them move deliberately over the uneven ground, Dumbo ears sweeping, and Sherlock noses vacuuming the forest floor. No smell is unimportant! With my limited senses and often preoccupied with the busy day ahead, I catch glimpses of the forest's story. Their noses read an entire novel, revealing who and what have gone before.

For twenty years I have performed this daily ritual in the company of several beloved dogs, including those of friends and neighbors. With Sherman and Chumley it is always a joy-filled adventure. Without them it would be just a walk.

SANDY HALE
Photographer

THERESA McKITTRICK
and TROOPER

~

THE PHONE RANG. It was my mom announcing that Trooper and I were going to be in the upcoming Mutt Derby she'd read about in the newspaper, and she'd do the driving.

It couldn't be denied that Trooper looks half greyhound, and I honestly thought we wouldn't be allowed to enter. His other half is collie, and happily none of the race officials turned us away. Feeling a little sheepish though, I avoided eye contact with the other owners, a few of whom muttered, "Oh no," but all in good fun.

There was a huge turnout. Dogs were separated by size and ran elimination heats as a crowd of laughing and cheering families and friends watched from the stands. Handlers held your dog on the starting line and owners stood about thirty yards away on the finish line. At the signal dogs were released to run straight to their owners. Wrong! The dogs had better ideas. Smart dogs ran for the pond, which looked cool and glistening in the hot sun. Friendly dogs knew a great social opportunity, and chased after each other in all directions. Confused canines either sat down or ran the wrong way. Trooper and several other dedicated dogs flew to their owners for a very close race, which Trooper won — thanks to the extent of his nose. And to his credit, he stopped when he got to me, unlike some.

When it came time for the grand finale, all who placed first lined up. It was a brilliant race, and the winner was the crowd favorite, an energetic, sweet brown dog. I like to think Trooper knew his greyhound traits gave him an unfair

advantage, and that his collie genes gallantly endowed him with the grace to place second — again by only a nose.

SUE ROGINSKI and DELLA

❧

I GRAB THE LEASH and ball. Della knows what's up. She gets excited and starts to bark. As far as she's concerned, we can't leave the house fast enough. We walk the six blocks to the park. As we get close, I let her off the leash. She heads straight for the park, turns around, and faces me. You see — she's waiting for the ball.

ELIZABETH GORELIK
Photographer

© 1995 Elizabeth Gorelik

ELANA HANSON and SHEENA

⌒

AS I HEADED to work at 5:30 one pitch-black winter morning, I was startled by a flash of white at the edge of my peripheral vision. Holding my breath, I opened the car door and slowly turned 360 degrees, wondering what sort of specter would pounce on me. Nothing happened. But when I stepped into the car, there in the passenger seat, grinning ear to ear, panting with tongue flopped out the side, was a pure white puppy about five months old. We already had a collection of five varied breeds and mutts, but what could I do? I turned and went back into the house with four big furry white feet at my heels. "Scot?" I whined, "we've got another dog."

SCOT SICKBERT
Photographer

NANCY COLE, WHITEY, ZAR, and CLEA

~

I LIVE AND WORK in the mountains of southern Oregon. There are three working dogs in our forestry crew. Whitey shoos squirrels and deer out of the garden and hawks from the bird feeder. He adores strangers. When he started licking and nuzzling a trespasser, I knew I needed Clea, a Great Pyrenees guardian dog.

Clea takes her work very seriously. She has a fine operatic bark. The neighborhood cougar hasn't visited the porch since she's been here. She discourages the teenagers who park Saturday nights below the house, barking incessantly from the moment they arrive. When they leave, she sighs dramatically and drinks about a gallon of water. Clea's done this informal tour of duty for Planned Parenthood since she was five months old.

Zar is a four-month-old Great Pyrenees puppy. He's a fuzzy, sixty-pound goof. He does what puppies do best — makes me laugh. He never met a stick he didn't want to carry, even if there's one already in his mouth. Once the whole crew stopped and held up a firewood truck to see if Zar could get a five-foot stick through a four-foot gate. We applauded when he did.

CHRISTOPHER BRISCOE
Photographer

LOUISE RAFKIN and LUCY

⌇

WHEN I WENT to get a puppy, I wanted a guarantee that it would grow up to be calm and gentle, a good athlete, obedient. The woman at the pound told me that the dog would do and be whatever I wanted, with the right kind of training. Still, I kept questioning. Will she catch a frisbee? Will she not run off? "It's up to you," the woman said. After six months of life with Lucy, I finally understand what she meant.

Raising a dog is like reliving your own childhood and parenting at the same time. I see Lucy's confusion when my limits change. I see her respond with appreciation when we have a regular routine. I see her react to my moods, shirk when I am angry, sulk when she doesn't get her way. In her eyes I see myself, my mother, and my father. I get tired, she gets tired, we push each other's buttons. (She puts the Frisbee in my hand and then snatches it away again quickly!) Then we're in each other's arms again. She puts up with my passion for dress-up and I indulge her with hours of belly rubbing. I got Lucy after losing another dog in a break-up, but she is the first dog that is really mine. Lucy is my teacher and I'm learning how to love.

MARIAN ROTH
Photographer

SUE COPPOLA, RIPLEY,
and YAGO

~

A S A POLICE K-9 trainer/handler for fifteen years, my life revolves around intelligent and talented dogs. It's been an honor and a privilege to work with such magnificent animals. They project tremendous joy doing their work, whether tracking a lost child, searching for hidden drugs, or putting their life on the line to protect their handler.

While some of the training is very serious, much is playful and can be entertaining for both dog and human. One of my most amusing memories comes from a K-9 comic student named Bear. Bear, a fourteen-month-old, 110-pound rottweiler, was being taught to surmount a six-foot-tall ladder. He made the ascent to the top, but only with a fair amount of coaxing with his favorite toy. As he started across the eight-foot-long catwalk, he froze in his tracks from fear of heights, and refused to use the dismount ramp. Standing at the bottom of the ramp, using his coveted toy, I attempted to motivate him to come down. Without warning, he took a mighty leap off the catwalk, flew through the air, totally clearing the ramp, and landed directly in the center of my chest, plowing me into the ground. He licked my face once, grabbed his reward, and trotted off to play. After catching my breath, I proceeded to laugh hysterically for several minutes. Of course, that was only until the pain set in.

BEN MACE
Photographer

A certified police K-9 (top) and a young dog in training

MARILYN McKNIGHT and HENRY
MADELINE A. McKENNA and CARA MIA
PAMELA A. KOKMEYER and NIKO
EDITH H. ROSS and RUSTY
MELISSA BERRYMAN and JETTA

~

FIVE YEARS AGO a few women dog-lovers met in a private home, upset by the deplorable conditions at the town's dog pound. We were anxious to do something, not only to improve the dogs' lives, but also to give them a second chance at life. The result of the meeting was the birth of a non-profit volunteer organization called the Friends of Falmouth Dogs.

The beautiful dogs in the photograph are all former pound residents, from more than 400 dogs given permanent, loving homes through the efforts of our group. Four of the women are volunteers, and the fifth is the new Animal Control Officer for the town.

Three hundred and sixty-five days a year, despite blizzards, hurricanes, heat waves, and holidays, volunteers spend a couple of hours caring for the dogs and preparing them for adoption. All the dogs are spayed or neutered and given veterinary care when necessary. Prospective homes are visited, dogs walked, groomed, and socialized, and follow-up visits made after each adoption.

Our goal is to build a shelter of our own someday that will accommodate more dogs than we now are able to handle.

BRENDA SHARP
Photographer

BECKY ROLLER, RUDY, and MAGGIE

～

They're spoiled rotten, my dollies, my babies. Oh, I know they're not
little people in fur jackets, they're enchanted pixies.

RICH AND BECKY ROLLER
Photographers

KRISTY CARLSON and SPENCER

❧

DON'T LET those long, delicious eyebrows fool you. Spencer's not as docile as he appears. The minute my boyfriend and I sit on the couch, he's between us. I've tried moving him next to me, but nothing works. Even when my girlfriend came over once to teach me how to two-step, Spencer was constantly underfoot, nipping at our heels. Possessive's not the word!

MICHELE PARKER
Photographer

On Location Photography

CLAUDIA M. TOKUYAMA-HACK, PUPPET E. YAN, HAPPY, and RUSSIAN BEAR

❧

IN THIS COUNTRY, my dogs and I are members of minority groups, yet, together, we represent the majority of the world's inhabitants. We wear our identities in our eyes and expressions, while we remain mute about our histories to those we do not know well. My dogs and I have funny ears and sweet eyes. We have all been lost, unwelcomed, and left behind, but have resilient spirits and share a zest for life that is complemented by our existence as a whole. We four are of mixed and proud heritages and form an unlikely but congenial pack.

My biggest regret is that one day too soon, this pack will leave one by one before me, to romp in the green meadows of heaven. It is my Asian nature to exist in the moment; to savor life as it unfolds. Yet, the Western influence in me can always look toward the future and realize that a tragedy is in the making; dogs' lives are so terribly short. Many people believe that dogs do not go to heaven, but I am not one of them. For, if heaven is a lovely place, then surely, it is graced by dogs. Most certainly, all of mine, past and present, will be among them. Of this I am certain. As usual, my dogs will all be wiggling, wagging, and waiting to greet me!

LESLIE J. CLOSE
Photographer

SHARON HOLLOWAY and BENNY

~

ALTHOUGH BENNY'S endless obsession with food is sometimes a bit hard to take, I am forever awed by the talent of his nose. One time he came charging down the driveway with an entire loaf of French bread in his mouth. I have no idea where he got it, and kept waiting for a neighbor to complain — but no one ever did.

BRENDA SHARP
Photographer

SARA BISHOP and JEZEPPIE

❧

MY HUSBAND and I were on our honeymoon, driving from Nebraska back to our home in Washington. We planned our activities with Zeppie, took hikes, swam in streams, and ordered room service instead of eating out. We did whatever it took so he wouldn't be left alone in a strange environment. One evening, however, my husband and I wanted a romantic dinner alone. As we left our hotel room, I felt little pleading brown eyes staring at my back. When I turned around, there was Zeppie looking at us through the window. We went back immediately and ordered room service.

ALAN REINEKE
Photographer

SHIRLEY E. BOYD and GUNNA B. BAD

◈

WHEN I WAS A CHILD I spent countless hours exploring the woods and fields surrounding my home. I loved the feeling of independence and freedom this brought me.

Then I became an adult. On a brisk autumn day, in only a moment, a stranger brought the realization to me that a woman alone in an uninhabited area could be very vulnerable.

I needed a companion who would enjoy running with me. The perfect solution was a sleek, black Doberman pinscher named Gunna.

Now I am free again to traverse the secluded, grassy trails and wander where I will.

CHERYL GRAVES CHAMBERS
Photographer

YUMIKO SATO and GABRIELA

~

O NCE WE ARRIVE at the park, Gabby runs off to find other dogs, smell things, and have fun. When she gets a certain distance from me, she stops suddenly and turns around to check in. Then she's off again, disappearing and reappearing magically out of nowhere. Gabby now has a little sister, Livia. When Livia was a baby and tired easily, I used to carry her in my tote bag so Gabby and I could have longer walks.

SHEL IZEN
Photographer

CINDY LOMBARDO and TENNYSON

~

After a long day at the office, we like to head for the open road.

VICKI LYNN THOMAS
Photographer

IRIS SELIG, BERT, and LULU

W HEN PEOPLE ASK what breed they are, I say they're industrial-strength Airedales with skunk breath, the new, improved size, or they're flat-backed aircraft terriers.

Lulu is joyful and athletic, and her son Bert is a big stuffed animal with genetically flawed ears. Mother and son love to chew on my chin and rough me up, especially after they've eaten tuna fish. They're singleminded, determined, and inclined to go AWOL during hunting season or on any moonlit night. One dawn we tracked them to a lake about a mile from our house, where we heard Lulu crying in distress on the far shore. When we whistled, they jumped right into the nearly frozen water, swam the half mile across, and sheepishly followed us home with icicles forming in their hair. They flopped down near the woodstove, slept for two days, and then left to go porcupine hunting.

I've come to believe that any dog I have becomes the dog I need.

They're my children-substitutes, and my love for them increases the longer we're together, and whenever I worry that I might lose them.

I know all the right places to scratch, and they get to sleep on the couch. After all, a dog's life is too short to worry about dirty furniture or fingernails.

DONNA RUTH CARUSO
Photographer

JANET KAHN and NAMO

∾

I ALWAYS KNEW I would live with another dog after Stellie died, but wondered how I would know the right one. I loved her so much, I couldn't really imagine a different dog. About a year and a half after her death I had a dream about a puppy whose face was so clear I knew I was supposed to look for him. When a friend said he dreamed about me and a puppy on the same night, I was convinced.

I began scouring the pounds, looking for the face in the dream. There were some great dogs, but they weren't the pup in the dream. Friends tried to assist, gave me information, offered pups from their dogs' litters, but nothing seemed right. Then one Sunday morning I woke from a dream with a voice talking in my ear. It said, clear as can be, "You must call the number on the slip of paper. There is only one puppy left. It is a male. He is yours, but he won't be there tomorrow." It was 7:00 A.M., a rude time to call anyone on Sunday morning, but I had to be somewhere quite early — and the voice had been so insistent.

After apologizing for waking them, I inquired about the puppies. "Well," said the woman, "there is only one left, and he is a male." My heart leapt into my mouth. "It is surprising that he is still here," she said. "Some friends were going to take him. . . ." We finished our conversation after they had given me a thorough dog-person interview. I hung up the phone and wept. In all the time looking through animal shelters, nothing had made me cry — not the cute little faces, nor the frustration from never finding the right pup, nothing. Yet this guy, whom I hadn't even met, somehow touched my heart.

ELLEN SHUB
Photographer

Namo: Sanskrit for homage, or great respect

KATY STRAUSS and LUCY

~

ROM THE MOMENT I saw Lucy walk from behind the MSPCA counter,
I loved her and told my mom she was the dog for me. I was adopting Lucy
to be an obedience dog for 4-H competitions, but she turned out to be my
best friend.

Although she's won many blue ribbons, you'd never guess it from the way she
acts at home. She's spoiled rotten, won't eat her food without people food on it,
and insists on sleeping right in the middle of my bed — thoughtfully providing me
the edge.

But Lucy isn't all spoiled. Whenever I get home she throws a fit — jumps up
and licks my face — no matter how short a time I've been gone.

BETH STRAUSS
Photographer

DONNASUE JACOBI and
LEO vom haus TYSON

～

L EO IS AN EXTREMELY intelligent working German shepherd dog — if
you think being an amateur comedian in the obedience ring is good work.
And how intelligent is Leo? He taught himself how to answer the tele-
phone. When it rings he makes a mad dash, slides over the hardwood
floors, yips with excitement, then bumps the phone off the cradle and barks into the
handset. I have a difficult time racing him for the phone — he runs with four legs, I
have two.

JOY REWICK
Photographer

RIVER KARMEN and MOLLY

~

OLD MOLLY DOG! You were a true pal for sixteen years. You stood by me as I fumbled through my twenties and then well into my thirties. And then somehow you became older than I. How did that happen? Toward the end of your life I used to wear you around my shoulders like a scarf when you'd suddenly become too tired to walk any further in the soft sand.

When you finally died, I buried you in the woods below my bedroom window. Your friend, Blue, (the gray tiger cat) missed you a lot. For weeks after you died, when I opened my eyes in the morning and looked out, I would see Blue holding vigil on a low branch of a pine tree directly above your grave. That got me more than anything. Rest in peace, my good friend.

L.E. McCAUSLAND
Photographer

ANN RICKARD, FALK, and KOA

〜

SWIMMING WITH my German shepherds, Koa and Falk, is an abiding joy in my life. We live in Hawaii near a beautiful lagoon where they love doing laps with me, retrieving coconut husks, and romping in the surf nearly every evening. Recently, on one of our sunrise walks, their preciousness was brought home to me.

I had stopped briefly to talk with friends. Meanwhile the boys were enjoying one of their favorite pastimes — hunting and chasing mongooses. As I turned to head home in the dense jungle, Falk, my seventy-pound puppy, was nowhere to be seen. Fighting panic, I searched for two hours in all directions, but to no avail. By then I was late for my volunteer work, gathering and arranging exotic flowers. Working with the beautiful bouquets of orchids, anthuriums, and gingers, I quieted my thoughts of sadness and confusion and focused on Falk's presence. Soon a picture of him grew in my mind, and I knew where he might be. I jumped in the truck and raced down the road to the spot I had seen in my mind's eye. Lo and behold, his sweet face was peering up at me from a seven-foot-deep, vine-covered lava crevice he had fallen into. Though I was shaken and cried tears of joy and relief, Falk seemed unfazed by his six-hour ordeal. Such a silly puppy.

REBECCA P. TINGLIN
Photographer

SARA KENNEDY and MR. WINSTON

 ~

URING THE HOLIDAY SEASON people can send a list to Santa in order to receive gifts. We decided to send our friends a different list itemizing each article our Mr. Winston has managed to devour in his short lifetime. After he chewed the bathroom floor, we said, "He's a puppy, he'll outgrow it." When he chewed holes in the wall, we decided to build a fence and keep him outside until he grew up. When he chewed the shingles on the house, we knew we were in trouble.

For all the critics who said to me over and over again, "Have you given him enough chewies?" read this!

One pair of slippers, three pairs of good
   shoes
One pair of rubber boots, one pair of
   sandals
One pair of snow boots
Two living room pillows, four regular
   pillows
Four sheets, one pillow sham, one
   comforter, four pillow cases
One L. L. Bean dog bed
Two boxes of Earl Grey tea, four boxes
   of pudding
One box of Glad bags, one bucket of
   cotton candy
Six rows of shingles on the porch at
   Martha's Vineyard
One row of clapboards in Framingham
Three blankets, countless socks

Four hats, from Australia, Ireland,
   Baltimore Orioles, etc.
One rug from South Africa, two scatter
   rugs
Four plastic wastebaskets
Two blouses, one pair of shorts
One London Fog coat, one overnight bag
One full vacuum bag
Two regular dog collars, two Promise
   collars, numerous leashes
Music tapes, one video tape
One bathroom floor, two big holes in the
   bathroom walls
One rubber mat, books, paint brushes
Gloves
Salt and pepper shakers
One box of Brillo pads, eight shampoo
   bottles, boxes of Kleenex

We rest our case. Forget the holidays. Mr. Winston is lucky to still be alive!

MARGIE ARNOLD
Photographer

LYNN HARRISON and BJ

~

THE FIRST TIME I saw BJ, she was an eight-week-old black fur ball bouncing around her master's yard with eleven siblings. I tormented myself with the decision. Should I bring such a being into my life? A month later I inquired about the availability of those twelve pups. "Yes, we have one still unspoken for, a female, second to the smallest and the liveliest of the litter."

The next two weeks were a rite of passage. This puppy turned my world upside down. I had had no idea what it would take to manage this bundle of energy, to fold her into my routine. The answer was that there could be no routine. Spontaneity ruled all our actions. I was in tears at least once a day, completely overwhelmed. And she made me laugh, and love.

BJ is now three years old, at once an enthusiastic athlete, a rascal, and an elegant young lady. I marvel at her life and what I imagine to be her outlook: We're here to have fun, aren't we?

CINDY CHOATE
Photographer

JO ANN METCALFE and COLE PORTER

~

I FIGURE COLE PORTER and I were meant to stick together for a long time. He was the dog I didn't want. . . . I had a million reasons why it wasn't the right time to bring something new into my life. The kids had all left the nest, I could travel more, and frankly, there was the matter of not wanting to go out in the cold at night with him.

But, following a successful campaign by my son and fiancé to get a dog into the household, I literally dropped everything to care for this loving black Lab. And Cole's arrival prompted me to stay home after planning to fly on a private jet to California with my fiancé and a friend. In the single most tragic event of my life, my fiancé perished in a plane crash on his trip to California.

As I struggle to cope with the sadness and loneliness from losing my loved one, my children and Cole Porter have been by my side. Beyond the adoration Labrador owners feels for their dog, I know in my heart and soul that I owe my life to Cole Porter.

JOHN CLIFFORD VAUGHAN
Photographer

ROBIN YOUNG, SANDINA, and TINA

～

TINA AND SANDINA are an odd couple. Tina is very old and sleeps all day. She has arthritis in her back legs and is going deaf. Her hangout is under the wisteria bush in the shade. The only time she acts alive is in the morning when it's time for her walk. Tina can look fierce at times, but really, she wouldn't hurt a fly.

Sandina is about six months old. She drives me crazy by pulling, and chewing on me, and peeing on the floor. She has the unique ability to transform herself into a hurricane at least three times a day. Sandina is sweetest when she's tired — that's when she'll curl up in my lap.

I love Tina because she is calm and affectionate. As for Sandina . . . well, like my mom says, she's worming her way into my heart.

ROBERT YOUNG
Photographer

© Robert Young

PAT de GROOT and ATISHA

~

I FIND IT HARD to say anything sensible about my dog, Atisha. I am her faithful loving servant and there is not much she can do to displease me. We do shout at each other now and then, but mostly we love each other passionately. I'm not sure, but I think she would like me to get her a dog for her birthday, though that might cause confusion since I do belong to her and she would have to share me.

TINA DICKEY
Photographer

ELEANOR LAZARUS, RIOJA, and CHIANTI

~

HAVING LEFT Rioja and Chianti outside in the little fenced-in yard behind my house, I called home to retrieve my messages. "Hello. This is Alex the barber, on Mount Auburn Street. I have 'Reggie' [Rioja] here. She's fine. We just ate the pizza I ordered for lunch. When can you come and get her?"

That was the first of many calls from Alex the barber. Each time I secured another suspicious-looking escape route in the fence — to no avail. My little wanderer was clearly motivated to get to her lunch date with Alex, and my patch jobs weren't deterring her one bit. Then I saw the impossible. Rioja and I were in the yard. I was raking, and when I looked up to find her — "Ahah!" She was three-quarters of the way up the five-foot chainlink fence, convict style, and over before I could reach her! I bring her to work now.

Her brother, Chianti, cares less for pizza than for chipmunks. His two front feet put a backhoe to shame. He can dig a homemade culvert four feet long in ten minutes flat. When I see nothing more than an ecstatically wagging tail, I know Chianti is on his way to China, hunting chipmunks.

My wanderer and my digger. Houdini and the Hunter. Erstwhile winos, Rioja and Chianti.

JANIS REDLICH
Photographer

98

SUSAN SELIGSON and LOUIE

~

M Y DOG'S FULL NAME is Lowtide Louie. He's something of a celebrity on the sand flats where we walk. His looks are unusual, kind of like a Lab that swallowed an exploding-hair pill. As all the dogs and their people who roam the flats know, Louie likes to keep moving. He despises idle human gossip and will stand nearby glaring, making harrumph noises, and seeming to glance at an imaginary watch where his wrist would be. If I go so far as to sit on the beach, he digs a hole under me. He is forever impatient to get downtown, because inside that insanely hairy head is a mental map of all his cookie stops: the bank, post office, pet shop, espresso bar. He pokes his head out at the bank drive-through to extract the biscuit himself, and he does the same thing at toll booths on the turnpike, mystified when he comes back empty-mouthed. What is most remarkable about Louie is his eyes, which are so penetrating and so human they have gotten us in trouble. For example, we were once in a Boston shop when a prissy elderly matron tapped me on the shoulder and said, "Oh Miss, your dog is staring at me."

BARBARA E. COHEN
Photographer

CHRISTINE AMATRUDO
and FANCY

~

WE RAISED MY DOG, Fancy, from a puppy for about a year and a half. She was not really ours. She was a Seeing Eye puppy. On November 6 I had to give her up. I was so sad. I would never forget her. I loved her a lot. Maybe she would be a guide dog for somebody who was blind.

Just a few days ago, we found out that she did not make it as a Seeing Eye dog. On Tuesday, November 22, my Dad finally said yes, I could take her back for my Christmas present! I was so happy to see her. Fancy came home for the holidays!

MARTHA EVERSON
Photographer

© Martha Everson

ALEXANDRA DAY, SPROCKET and ZABALA

~

EIGHTEEN YEARS AGO, when my husband and I moved our family to the country, we chose (from books) two breeds of dogs to buy — an Irish terrier and a rottweiler. Since our profession was book making, both dogs found their way into books — the rottweiler became *Good Dog, Carl,* and the Irish terrier was Paddy in *Paddy's Payday*. Aside from the books, the dogs were so woven into our family that we stuck to those breeds in succeeding years. The Irish terrier, Cornelius Sprocket McGillicuddy (named for Connie Mack, but called "Sprocket") and Zabala, our current "Carl," are as much a part of our life and work as were the originals.

Now that my children are in their twenties, Sprocket and Zabala have the additional job of taking the place of small children around the house. They do their best — are messy, funny, demanding attention and loving. Also they pose for me when I need them to model, sleep as close to me as possible, and accompany me anywhere they're allowed.

I often travel and make public appearances with Zabala. At a recent book signing in Ohio our session ran late, and we were leaving the store the same moment the next event was starting. I wasn't holding Zabala's leash — I often don't, because our communication is so good we can navigate hotel lobbies, airports, and even crowds of screaming children with just words. As we passed the raised area where the appearances were being held, the bookstore manager finished her introduction and said, "And now, here's Michael Feinstein." With perfect

©1995 Erin Spencer

timing, Zabala walked up the stairs and presented himself. Naturally it brought down the house, and, fortunately, Michael Feinstein was laughing, too.

ERIN SPENCER
Photographer

BONNIE BERGIN
with service dog hopeful

~

I CREATED AND PIONEERED the concept of the service dog: a dog that turns light switches on and off, picks up dropped or needed items, pulls wheelchairs, and opens doors, literally and figuratively, for people with disabilities. Kerry Knaus was the first disabled individual willing to get involved with what she later confided to me was "this crazy lady's idea." At nineteen, Kerry would do anything that might enhance her life. What she didn't know then is that a significant part of that life, starting with Abdul, the first service dog (her partner for sixteen years), and extending through most of those sixteen years would be consumed helping me develop the concept.

After years of experimentation, numerous mistakes, and some successes, it became evident that Labs and golden retrievers make the best service dogs. The importance of starting from puppyhood also became evident, since those early months are a crucial part of the dog's development. Habits learned early are deeply ingrained, and next to impossible to change.

Now, over twenty years later, close to one hundred service dog programs are at work throughout the world bringing independence and canine companionship to people with disabilities. I'm concentrating my efforts on improving the field and sharing that knowledge so still more people can benefit.

The service dog: a working partnership that provides the unconditional love and acceptance we all so desire.

ROY CROCKETT
Photographer

SUZY BECKER and WYLIE
the World's Best Dog

❧

My dog doesn't have bad breath when she wakes up and I like the smell of her feet. I've never said that about anybody I slept with before.

JANET KNOTT
Photographer

© 1995 Janet Knott

CYNTHIA FOSTER and CHARLIE

～

I'VE ALWAYS ADORED DOGS and for a short time bred the enormous and magnificent Great Pyrenees in the United States and, later, here in Provence. *Oui,* I love dogs; still, when my husband discovered a litter of tiny poodles displayed in the trunk of an old Renault at a French horse fair, I resisted. Did I really want a poodle?

Many years later, with all my other dogs gone, it's still my little girl, Charlie, who warms my heart, reads my mind, and accompanies me everywhere, including the best restaurants in France.

CATHRYN GRIFFITH
Photographer

MARY De ANGELIS and GABE

❧

I AM AN AUNT to a Lab named Gabe. He stays with me about a week a month, when his mom is busy or away. I get to be the good aunty, have tons of fun with him, give him whatever he wants to eat, play stick with him for hours, and take him for long walks. He can even sleep on my bed, something he can't do at home.

When Gabe arrives, both my partner and I get really excited; we grow attached to him, and when he goes we really miss him. Then we continue with our lives and realize we could never have a dog full-time; we're just too busy. But suddenly it's time for Gabe to come back to the fun house and we're excited all over again! They say it takes a village to raise a child. I think it's the same with a dog.

BARBARA E. COHEN
Photographer

MAUREEN A. FREDRICKSON
and GAIBHNE

~

GAIBHNE AND I visit children who have been abused. His ability to iden-tify the most needy kids is as uncanny as it is accurate. When we enter the nursery or classroom, he searches for children who linger outside the group, too afraid or withdrawn to join. The staff and I watch as he lowers himself to lie beside them. In situations with very sad children, he gazes calmly into their faces, and then exquisitely touches the tip of their nose with the tip of his tongue. When they squeal with delight, he remains gentle and pants quietly.

Recently Gaibhne surprised me again with his special gift. Raising his head from snoozing, he stared after a woman who had come into my office for directions to the resource center. Then he got up from his bed, followed her, and returned in fifteen minutes. Later that day the resource center director stopped by my office. She told me Gaibhne had come into the center, stood next to the woman, and stared at her. He nudged the woman's hand with his nose until she stopped reading and hugged him. As she was leaving, she told the director that her dog had just died the week before.

JERRY DAVIS
Photographer

ROBIN KOVARY and AVA

~

FOR YEARS Ava resembled a friendly, spring-loaded, ball-catching rhinoceros. She had only two gears — high and off (sleeping mode). Fortunately, after nine years, she's developed a quiet, contemplative side. We often sit together on my front stoop and contentedly watch passersby. There are few moments more peaceful than those nuzzling Ava's soft warm muzzle, or stroking her big, beautiful ears.

HAROLD FEINSTEIN
Photographer